TABLE OF CONTENTS

BEING A SUCCESSFUL BROKER 3
   What Is A Broker 3
   History of Brokers 3
   Types of Broker 5
   Difference Between Broker and Trader 5
   The Broker as An Intermediary Company 7
   The Broker as An Individual Specialist 8
   Qualities of A Great Broker 8
   How to Be A Successful Broker 12
      Five Requirements to Be A Broker 12
      What Must You Study to Be A Broker? 14
      Six Fundamental Traits of a Successful Broker 15
   The Broker's Mindset: 10 keys to success 17
   How to Help in Supporting Financial Needs 21

THE BASICS ABOUT THE STOCK MARKETS 24
   Stock Market Law 24
      Law No. 1: Buy When Others Sell 25
      Law No. 2: Keep 30% Of Your Funds Always Available.. 25
      Law No. 3: Calculate the Real Value of The Stock Without Being Fooled (As Everyone Does) By the Price 26
      Law No. 4: Control Budgets 27
      Law No. 5: Varies in Several Sectors, But Be Careful! 27
      Law No. 6: Choose A Maximum Of 10 Titles 29
      Law No. 7: Think Long-Term 29
   What Category of Training Is Required to Become A Stockbroker? 30
   Responsibilities of A Broker in The Stock Market 34

What Work Does It Take to Be A Stockbroker? 35

specifications to Be A Stockbroker 36

Types of Advisory Positions for A Stockbroker 39

Next Degree of Banking 39

Five Tips to Learn to Fund into The Stock Market for
Beginners 40

THE WORLD OF CRYPTOCURRENCIES 44

GENESIS of Cryptocurrency 46

Types of Cryptocurrencies 48

The Main Characteristics of Cryptocurrencies 52

Correlations Between Cryptocurrency and Broker 54

How to Invest in Cryptocurrencies: Watch Out Volatility! . 56

   The 5 Golden Rules for Investing in Cryptocurrency 56

How Academics Invest in Crypto-Currency 59

Steps in Finding Cryptocurrency Broker 59

THE NEWBORN CHINESE DIGITAL YUAN 61

What Is China's Digital Currency? 61

Origin of the DCEP 63

Objectives of the DCEP 65

The Technology Behind the DCEP How Does the Chinese
Digital Currency Work? 67

Legality in China and The Rest of The World 68

China and The Need for A Digital Currency for Its Nation .. 69

Characteristics of China's Digital Currency 70

Scope and Consequences of The DCEP For China 75

The Benefits of Virtual Currency for China 75

China's Fight Against the US 76

GLOSSARY 79

BEING A SUCCESSFUL BROKER

WHAT IS A BROKER

A broker is an individual or institution that organizes transactions between a buyer and a seller in specific sectors in exchange for a commission when the transaction is executed. The agent acts as a broker or intermediary between a buyer and a seller, usually taxing a commission and becoming a director of the agreement. He is also in charge of advising and advising on business-related issues. The practice of the broker trade usually requires a license.

A broker is an agent or company responsible for executing the purchase or sale of financial instruments that its clients request. Their primary activity is to act as an intermediary between their clients and the market, finding a seller when their client gives them a purchase order or giving them a sell order.

In general, a broker is a self-reliant agent widely used in some industries. The primary responsibility is to bring in sellers and buyers, and therefore a broker is a third-party arranger between a buyer and a seller. An example could be a real estate broker facilitating the sale of a property. Brokers can also provide considerable market information on prices, products, and market conditions. A broker can speak to either the seller (90% of the time) or the buyer (10%), however not both simultaneously. An example could be a stockbroker, which makes the purchase or sale of securities on behalf of its client. Brokers play a fundamental role in the sale of stocks, bonds, and other financial services.

HISTORY OF BROKERS

The first Brokers appeared in the 12th century in France. The "Courratiers de Change" was in charge of managing and regulating the debts of farming communities on behalf of the banks. Some sources suggest that the word broker comes from the English "break" (break) but comes from the French word "brocour."

According to this theory, brochureur was a wine retailer, acquiring barrels and selling their contents by glasses, using a drill bit to drill them. This term, which appears documented for the first time from the thirteenth century, would designate agents and stockbrokers since 1700. Throughout the 20th century, the significant expansion of this sector took place. Coinciding with the different contraction periods and rise in the stock markets, the profession was also changing. Without going any further, in the sixties, a division between brokers became popular that somehow continues to this day.

On the one hand, traditional brokers sought to attract their clients with a wide range of services and privileged access to stock information. While the so-called Discount Brokers concentrated on cheap and straightforward trading, carrying out buy and sell orders with a reduced commission, but without providing investment advice. Accompanied by aggressive marketing, Discount Brokers managed to create a significant market niche. Within the brokers' history in the eighties, the first online brokers entered the market through General Electrics, Information Exchange Network. Online or internet trading, however, would not take off until well into the nineties.

It was radically transforming the stock market industry, where companies such as Emporio Trading have become unmatched benchmarks today. The truth is that the revolution that the internet has brought about in many economic sectors has been no less so in this field. The creation of infinite networks that spread to all corners of the globe and, above all, the making available of an enormous amount of information have favored the emergence of a whole body of brokers that can operate efficiently and with fewer costs Transaction.

TYPES OF BROKER

- Energy agent
- Franchise agent
- Real estate agent
- Customs broker
- Insurance broker: Person who acts as an intermediary for several insurance companies, marketing insurance contracts to their clients.
- Stockbroker (financial, business, or exchange): Person who advises or carries out transactions of variable income and securities in financial markets.
- Forex broker
- Bookmaker: the person who takes bets and mediates between bettors.
- Travel agent: Person who sells, advises, and manages the logistics of trips contracted by their clients.
- Talent agent: A person who acts as an intermediary between sports or entertainment workers and an employer.
- Shipbroker

DIFFERENCE BETWEEN BROKER AND TRADER

Brokers and traders are two categories of major players in the international financial markets, and they sell and buy financial instruments. But there are significant differences between their roles.

A trader is a person who makes the purchase and sale of financial instruments on his account. The trader is the investor and demands the figure of the Broker (the intermediary with the market) to finish the purchase and sale operations that he requests. Therefore, all traders must open an account with a broker in charge of implementing the procedures.

Theoretically, there is no need for training or accreditation. But you must have knowledge and skills so as not to lose money. The trader launches buy or sell orders in the market but do not have free access to these markets; he needs an intermediary to give it to him and execute his orders. This is the Broker.

The Broker gives the trader the exchanging stage and a broad assortment of analysis instruments, value history, different sorts of diagrams, examination pointers, volume adding machines, monetary news, and so on.

There are different types of traders depending on their trading strategies and the period in which they usually keep their operations open, from scalpers (who operate in brief periods of minutes or even seconds), day traders (who open and close their operations within the same day), swing traders (who keep their trades open for days or even weeks) to traders who trade long-term for months or even years.

It Will Help If You Have It in Mind That:

- The trader is the broker's client. He makes the investment decisions.
- The trader launches the orders in the market; the Broker executes them.
- The trader collects the profits or assumes the loss of the orders launched in the markets. The Broker receives his commission, regardless of the result of the executed order.
- The trader makes his trading decisions based on the technical or fundamental analysis he performs and his style: scalping, intraday, or long-term trading.
- There cannot be a broker since their activity's object would not exist if there is no trader.

THE BROKER AS AN INTERMEDIARY COMPANY

Brokers, as organizations, give added benefit since they can give market information and studies. Brokers can be either the dealer or the purchaser, however by and large not both. Purchasing and selling budgetary instruments is basically incomprehensible without a merchant's administrations, which offers monetary business sectors access. Specialists must have the assets and instruments to arrive at the broadest conceivable base of purchasers and dealers. They at that point channel these shrouded sellers or buyers to locate the ideal match between their terms.

Then again, a sole ownership, particularly one new to the market, will probably not have similar association with customers as a representative.

Another advantage of utilizing a broker is cost: they can be more affordable in more unassuming business areas, with more modest records, or with a limited extent of things.

THE BROKER AS AN INDIVIDUAL SPECIALIST

If we speak of the Broker as a specialist, it is also considered an intermediary between a seller and a buyer. It is found, in particular, within the large brokerage companies, whether or not they have a bank or an investment finance company behind them.

The Broker function facilitates operations between different clients by identifying the best price, quantity, and delivery conditions for a specifically requested product.

QUALITIES OF A GREAT BROKER

How might you tell a reputable business broking organization from an awful one? The relevant inquiry ought to be: can you honestly tell a decent business broking office from a terrible one? Indeed, you surely can; however, it's not generally that simple. Nonetheless, there are unquestionably characteristics that differentiate the excellent business broking office from the terrible one, and these characteristics are very noticeable to the individuals who focus. A portion of these are:

- **Severe Adherence to Ethics:**

The essential contrast between a reputable business broking organization and an awful one is that the previous carefully hold fast to morals. At the same time, the last frequently shows an absence of morals. Like every other expert, there are the odd ones out among business representatives, and the lack of morals in some business intermediaries is a reality, however, a disastrous one. Another inappropriate thing is that there is no simple method of testing a business broking office's moral. The ideal path is to ensure that you pick business merchants who are individuals from some industry body, for example, the AIBB, and so forth. That is because business dealers who are individuals from an industry body consent to carefully cling to the body's Standards of Professional Conduct just as its Code of Ethics.

Some may contend that simple acknowledgment of a code doesn't ensure anything. Valid, however, at any rate, it's a beginning stage and a decent one at that. Something else you can do is to request customer tributes and check references. However, customer tributes and references may not generally present a genuine picture. You can depend on being given honors from and references to the most fulfilled customers – customers who will have valuable comments about the office.

The third route is to check with your bookkeeper and lawyer or different bookkeepers and lawyers, you may know. That is because independent venture deals exchange essentially include lawyers and bookkeepers and these experts are a magnificent wellspring of references to moral business broking offices. The lawyers and bookkeepers you know may not be engaged with private company deals exchanges as such experts will in general practice nowadays. However, they may know or might have the option to discover bookkeepers or lawyers who are associated with such interactions and can, in this manner, allude to a presumed and moral business broking office.

- **Transparency and Honesty:**

A decent business broking office has an overall demeanor of receptiveness and trustworthiness, while a terrible one typically needs such air. You may not generally have the option to distinguish this air, yet as a rule, you can depend on your gut to give you some sign after you meet with or converse with somebody at the organization. There are sure notice signs that animate your hunch and decide its bearing. For example, was the individual you met with or conversed with avoiding your inquiries through and through or giving vague answers? Is it safe to say that he was or she ready to plunk down with you and answer every one of your inquiries to the best of their capacity? If not, why not? Was it because the office had something to cover up? A certifiable and legitimate business broking organization doesn't have anything to stow away; thus, when you visit or call, they will plunk down with you and answer every one of your inquiries in the most immediate way and as much detail as you require.

- **Capacity to Correctly Value a Business:**

Demanding adherence to ethics and straightforwardness and dependability are huge, yet what use is a good and authentic business broking association in case they are not handy enough to offer the kinds of help you require – the hugest being the correct valuation of your business. Your business must be valued effectively. If your business is overrated, you won't have the option to sell it. On the other, if it is underestimated, it will sell quickly. However, you won't have the option to make a benefit on the deal.

Have a conversation with a planned business broking office about valuation and ask them how they would esteem your business if you chose to work with them. Do some light perusing on the three distinct sorts of approaches to have the option to check their fitness here. Moreover, request tests of their estimating examinations. They ought to have the opportunity to give conventional examples. Take the samples with you and experience them. Check whether their examination would interest you enough to consider getting it if you were keeping watch for such a business. Your bookkeeping or budgetary arranging foundation should make it extremely simple for you to survey the examples.

- **Capacity to Develop and Implement an Effective Marketing Strategy**:

A decent business broking office can create and actualize a viable promoting technique to rapidly and productively sell your business. Ask representatives at the planned office about the showcasing methodology they have at the top of your business's priority list. On the off chance that, also as can be normal, you are posting it on the web can't publicize your business reasonably in light of the fact that you can list your business online in isolation. So why trouble to pay them? A nitty-gritty conversation with merchants at the imminent office on this issue ought to be sufficient to assist you in deciding whether they can adequately advertise your business or not.

- **Imperative Education and Experience**:

Agents at a reputable business broking organization have the imperative training and experience, yet continuously put resources into their schooling and expert turn of events. Like some other expert, a decent business agent needs to stay aware of current industry patterns, government guidelines, new valuing approaches, advertising methodologies, and so on.

- **Relationship building abilities:**

Relationship building abilities aren't just one of the main characteristics that different dealers at a reputed business organization from those at a terrible one, yet also one of the most obvious ones. The briefest of gatherings with the forthcoming agent are sufficient to let you know whether the individual in question has this quality. Furthermore, imagine a scenario where the agent isn't happy to meet you face to face. All things considered, if the specialist isn't eager to take that much time and put forth that much attempt, would you be able to anticipate that such an agent should invest sufficient energy into selling your business? Clearly, not. If the agent can't intrigue you, odds are the person has a low impact on purchasers. Also, you can generally anticipate that such a merchant should effortlessly sell your business, can you?

HOW TO BE A SUCCESSFUL BROKER

Becoming a broker is not something that takes a couple of days. To be a stockbroker, you will need to have a series of essential knowledge and skills to function as a fish in the water.

To successfully carry out your work as a broker, you can be certified through training. A brokerage training generally consists of three steps: first, the Basic Theory Valuer, then different theory about your desired specialization, and finally, a practical part focused on your field. After that, you will have to recertify every five years to keep the certificates.

FIVE REQUIREMENTS TO BE A BROKER

A broker is an intermediary agent in financial operations that receives a commission for its intervention. Despite the risks and stress involved in performing, it is one of the most money-earning jobs. Without a doubt, this is the occupation that many aspire to thanks to the high commissions and the expensive life that comes with it, but dedicating yourself to this profession requires hard preparation and a willingness to work rigid day-to-day basis. It is not enough to be passionate about finances, and it is not enough to be good with numbers. A broker must meet or adopt the following characteristics to be successful:

1. **Have Excellent Financial Training**
   It is not the only requirement, but it is basic. You don't need a college degree to work as a broker, but broker-dealers prefer trained people. A bachelor's degree in Mathematics, Business Administration, or Economics provides a good foundation of financial training to get you started in this world. And companies highly value having an MBA.

2. **English Proficiency**
   The financial world speaks the Saxon language. The markets are international, and fluid relationships are established with people from all over the world at a hectic pace, so a broker must be able to do well in this language to mindful of what is happening around him.

3. **Commercial Skills**
   To get a portfolio of the right clients. Having previous experience as a commercial or possessing sales skills helps this profession get a good portfolio of clients to advise on investing or buying.

4. **High Resistance to Stress**
   Being decisive adds extra points. The stockbroker is continually under pressure, requiring him to know how to control his nerves and deal with the focus of a profession that demands a lot of time and dedication.

Being decisive and having good emotional intelligence score points when it comes to success in this profession require significant control.

5. **National Securities Market Commission**
   The first step is to officially register. The National Securities Market Commission is a public body that depends on the Secretary of State for the Economic and supervises Spain's securities markets. If all the above qualifications are met, this is undoubtedly the first step that must be taken to enter this professional world.

WHAT MUST YOU STUDY TO BE A BROKER?

Most brokers have a career and went to college; it is essential to have a college degree to be a stockbroker. But you will have an obligation to pass a series of exams that will authorize you to practice this career. It would be perfect if you also kept in mind that most brokerage houses and financial institutions prefer to hire traders, brokers, and agents with the knowledge and university degrees.

University careers related to the business of stocks and shares.

All financial-related college majors can drive you to be a stockbroker or stockbroker. You must have diverse abilities. Some careers that can help you become a broker:

- Business Administration
- Economy
- Public accounting
- Commercial administration
- Industrial relationships
- Economic engineering

- Mathematics
- Statistics
- Marketing
- International Trade
- Financial law

Other professionals are not graduating of university degrees related to the financial field and can break into the leading stock exchanges on the planet, such as London and Tokyo.

It won't matter if you have a history degree or are an educator. Knowing about the markets' behavior, mastering the numbers, and some charisma, you can exercise this exciting career.

SIX FUNDAMENTAL TRAITS OF A SUCCESSFUL BROKER

The following six traits will help the Broker or mediator to be ready in this sector:

1. **Passionate:** Successful insurance brokers are passionate about what they do. They like to help others prepare for the unexpected. They believe in what they sell. They must have a mission to improve the lives of their current and potential customers. Your services can have a significant impact on the lives and legacies of your clients.

2. **Outgoing:** The brokers must be pleasant and able to make their customers feel comfortable.

3. **Assimilate Rejection:** They will face a large number of rejections, especially early in their careers. Many clients

will postpone meetings and decisions without us waiting. We must not get discouraged; with a good follow-up, we will finally get the desired response.

4. **Have Defined Objectives:** brokers and intermediaries must establish their business objectives in the short, medium and long term. In this way, they will continuously be on the alert, facing the usual business challenges.

5. **Organized:** A good broker must analyze his production and administrative tasks. Properly following up with your clients optimizes the relationship between them, allowing brokers to offer a better service. Success requires persistence.

6. **Good Listeners:** brokers must pay full attention to their potential clients' concerns, which will enable them to satisfy their needs.

THE BROKER'S MINDSET: 10 KEYS TO SUCCESS

Financial markets have the peculiarity of having two elements that make people uncomfortable; one is uncertainty, and the other is probabilities. Both factors are destabilizing agents from the personal point of view because we have the innate characteristic of controlling everything (to be protected and have security), but this does not work in the markets.

A person who wants to commit himself to the financial markets and obtain recurring profits will have to save time and effort to create a mentality according to the ups and downs that the needs propose every day.

To face and participate in the market, a broker must have an extreme, flexible mentality and a high degree of humility because the demand is maximum but even more so, the internal obstacles that appear in each of us

A broker with a mentality that contains that indispensable quota of humility and is healthy will manage his inner saboteurs, such as the uncertainties and questions that the market poses at all times. Also, having mental clarity will allow you to make decisions with confidence because if you hesitate or doubt, the market will take you out of the way. So far, it has been clear that to operate in the financial markets; it is necessary to change the mentality, which means having clarity, strength and humility. I imagine you are wondering: how do you build such a mind? To achieve this, it is necessary to work on ten key elements:

1. **Self-Knowledge:**
The key and vital point, if you don't know who YOU ARE, what you want for your life, why do you trade, what YOU

ARE very good at, what you should improve at, what talents you have and what you are passionate about; you will live in a permanent question mark, which will take you around the same place.

2. **Clear Rules:**
   If you want to stay in the markets, you will need to create clear regulations both at an operational and emotional level; And of course, making them is not enough, but you must apply them in a disciplined way.

3. **Ego Management:**
   Priority and fundamental this point. You must have perfect control of your ego (we have all of this agent) because otherwise, it will be impossible for humility to dwell in your mind. When doing business, a broker is dominated by his ego runs severe risks of losing everything.

4. **Accept You:**
   One of the keys to having a clear and healthy mind is knowing how to accept yourself as YOU ARE because this will take a lot of emotional pressure off you and allow you to put yourself in the right place. Not denying yourself is an excellent step towards your personal and professional success.

5. **Learn to Lose:**
   If you want to make a living from being a broker, this is one of the first things you should learn, since, in our life, no one has taught us to lose money and above all that you should not lose emotional control when this happens. When you learn to lose by measuring risks, your mind acquires a significant mental strength.

6. **Take It as A Long-Distance Race:**
   Prepare your mind as if you are running a marathon and not a 100-meter race. This is one of the big mistakes of many traders; they want to make a lot of money quickly, which leads them to skip stages. And when this happens, the market sooner or later puts you in your place with a lot of pain.

7. **Know the Risk You Take:**
   Transmit to your mind what chance you are willing to assume in each operation based on your capital because when you are clear about this, you act within the market with peace of mind, knowing that if you lose, your financial world will not fall.

8. **Reflect and Meditate:**
   Reflecting much helps your mind filter information, discard the one that does not work and record the one that does. Also, make friends with meditation, spend a few minutes relaxing and renewing your inner energy through meditation.

9. **Make Your Own Decisions:**
   It is better to be mistaken for your decisions than for the advice of others. When you get used to making your own decisions and taking responsibility for them, you will be giving your mind security and confidence, regardless of the result obtained.

10. **Eliminate Attachments:**
    Attachments are presented in various ways, but one that predominates in trading is the attachment to the outcome. The best way to separate it from your operations is by focusing on the process and on what you must do at all times.

When you do this, your mind will be stable, and the positive results will come of their own accord. These ten elements will allow you to have a clear, humble and healthy mind, which will enable you to confront with guarantees the uncertainty, fear and greed that the markets propose every day.

HOW TO HELP IN SUPPORTING FINANCIAL NEEDS

A Broker will help you obtain an SME Credit: Indeed, at some point in your life, you have needed the support of a loan. Whether to buy a house, to go on a trip, to take advantage of a promotion, to invest in your business or to cover an unexpected situation.

Credit can be generous support, especially when you have opportunities along the way where you need capital to continue moving forward. And if we speak in the specific case of a business or company, even more so, a line of credit is going to be essential to support its growth.

The bank is the most common place where you can request a loan of any kind, but what happens when you have problems obtaining it? This happens to many people; they approach one, two or three different bank options, and none of them give them a YES for an answer. They do not even understand why the rejection?

In that case, the perfect recommendation is to look for a trusted Broker who will help you with their knowledge and advice to identify the real problem that is occurring and thus understand if your credit application can be approved or not.

A Financial Broker's task to help you obtain a loan lies in the analysis of your profile and your objective to determine the possibility of authorization of a loan in the bank before the integration of any document.

All financial institutions have different policies for the qualification of a credit application. Therefore, you may be spending too much time figuring out which one is right for you or which can give you the closest approval to what you want to achieve.

For this reason, these are ten ways in which a broker can help you obtain an SME loan:

1. **Know your market and can give you good recommendations:** There are brokers significant time in various sorts of financial items. Choose the one with the perfect reputation or provide you with as much information as possible to decide more assertively.

2. **Analyzing your current situation generates alternative solutions:** The only way to clarify a problem is by identifying it and understanding what is causing it. Therefore, for your economic situation to improve, you must speak the truth with your Broker, since this way, he can give you the best credit alternative that solves your case.

3. **It saves you time and effort in the search for a loan:** In a meeting, you will know the different offers that financial institutions give you to cover your needs without visiting each one.

4. **It shows you comparisons in the different financial products:** Your Broker will expose you to a financial analysis comparing the best options that exist for you; this in a way that you understand the benefits and advantages that you obtain between one or another credit alternative.

5. **It has alliances that benefit you and facilitate the credit process:** The process of a loan is part of the life of your Broker. Therefore indeed, it already has the

necessary and suitable contacts that will help you to give great ease and agility to your credit process.

6. **It helps you negotiate better credit conditions in your favor:** Because its main objective is to see your interests, the Broker of your choice must-see for your interests and thus give you an excellent experience.

7. **He advises you financially and gives you feedback on how you manage your finances:** To maintain a healthy financial life, your credit broker must provide you with post-financing strategies to improve your financial habits.

8. **Your attention is personalized, and you do not favor any bank or financial institution:** Remember here that you are the customer and the main objective is to live a great experience. First of all, the service with your trusted Broker must be personalized and impartial so that the best option can be objectively defined based on your needs and your goals.

9. **He is always ready to answer any questions and attend to your credit concerns:** A broker accompanies you throughout the credit process, understanding that the client is not used to or has information on the complete experience of applying for a loan. Communication is essential and very important to feel safe during the time that the operation takes.

10. **You can pay him for his services until you see the result of his work:** The payment of a broker's service is based on its results, so you can rest easy since it is unnecessary to pay the full cost from the beginning. An

agreement or negotiation can be reached that is convenient for both parties.

With this, we now have better understanding why having a Broker can help you and be very useful to process a credit. "A Financial Broker can see what others do not see."

THE BASICS ABOUT THE STOCK MARKETS

In finance, the stock market is the place, not necessarily physical, where equities are traded. This market is divided into primary and secondary. Newly issued shares are placed on the primary market, while securities already in circulation are traded on the secondary market. The issuing companies, therefore, raise new financial resources only through the primary market.

STOCK MARKET LAW

Every Professional Investor knows and always respects the 7 Laws of the Stock Market that must never be ignored, and if you want to survive in these markets too, you must learn them by heart:

1. Buy when others sell
2. Keep 30% of your funds always available.
3. Calculate the real value of the stock without being fooled (as everyone does) by the price
4. Check budgets
5. Vary across multiple sectors, but be careful!
6. Choose a maximum of 10 titles.
7. Think long term

LAW NO. 1: BUY WHEN OTHERS SELL

A real investor does not get scared when the world stock exchanges collapse due to some macroeconomic news. On the contrary, he is often happy because he can buy back at a significantly discounted price the shares of companies, he already had in his equity portfolio. The more people panic and sell, the more the professional investor buys.

Once "the sheep," or the people who are influenced by the media, understand that the situation is not as tragic as it seemed (the significant shareholders of the media make us big money like this: SPREAD FALSE NEWS AROUND TO DROP THE PRICE OF AN EXCELLENT COMPANY TO BE ABLE TO BUY IT AT RIPPED PRICES AND MAKE A FALSE PROPAGANDA OF GARBAGE COMPANIES TO BE ABLE TO RAISE THE PRICE TO THE STARS AND THEN SELL AS IF THERE WERE NO TOMORROW THAT POOR COMPANY IN THE HANDS OF THE CHICKENS). And prices start to rise again; then they too begin to buy back, with the only difference that professional investors had bought at bargain prices (when everyone was afraid and were selling excellent stocks at low prices). At the same time, beginners have purchased at a much higher price than the professional investor.

LAW NO. 2: KEEP 30% OF YOUR FUNDS ALWAYS AVAILABLE.

Having 30% of your funds ready to use gives us a competitive advantage over beginners for two reasons: It allows us to buy the same stock even at lower prices by averaging a higher purchase price with a lower one. Consequently, when that stock goes up again, it is as if you had bought it at an even lower price, increasing even more—more your earnings.

You have the opportunity to buy the shares of one or more companies that suddenly become attractive. In this way, you do not miss out on golden opportunities because you had no more funds to invest. If you are wondering if liquidating one or more good companies to have the funds available in the case of a golden opportunity is a good idea, no, it's not a very good idea, the question arises: why liquidate an excellent company, healthy, secure and competitive that is part of your portfolio? Remember to keep 30% of your funds ready to use because you never know when you might need them, and if you lose a good deal just because you don't have the funds available, I assure you that you will eat your hands.

LAW NO. 3: CALCULATE THE REAL VALUE OF THE STOCK WITHOUT BEING FOOLED (AS EVERYONE DOES) BY THE PRICE

One of the dumbest mistakes that most of those who play at investing make are to think that price and value are the same. Nothing more wrong! The price represents nothing more than how much the company's stock is trading at that exact moment. STOP! He doesn't give us any other information about the future of that company.

Instead, the real value of the action is a whole other thing. The Professional investor, before buying the shares of a company, calculates the value of the claim does not stop at a price. He goes much deeper, as the cost is nothing more than the intrinsic entity of the share, that is how much it is worth mathematically that particular title. A company could have a high price and a low value and vice versa, so always be careful not to misunderstand these two terms.

LAW NO. 4: CONTROL BUDGETS

You can't be an investor in the stock markets if you've never seen a balance sheet. If you are part of those who have seen the movie "Wall Street" and you want to play as an investor without having to be bored studying for hours and hours a budget, then forget it. This world is not for you. So why analyze the balance sheet? Simple, in this way you will know if a company is attractive or not. I'll give you a stupid example (indeed, very stupid, but I need it to make you understand the concept). Could you tell me if a shop "earns a lot" (I'll leave you the yardstick of how much "a lot" is)? Of course, you can imagine, it certainly doesn't take a top: Turnover-Expenses-Taxes-.... = Net profit!

How did you calculate it? You walked past the store and said: "BUY!" like in the movie "Wall Street"? Of course not, I guess. You did a mini-analysis, and you found that that shop (after expenses, taxes, everything removed...) has an excellent percentage of net profit compared to turnover. I can assure you that it also applies to large companies, but there are many more factors in between. So, if you live in films, go back to earth, the reality is very different!

LAW NO. 5: VARIES IN SEVERAL SECTORS, BUT BE CAREFUL!

If you think that all sectors are suitable investments, you are very wrong; some are more dangerous than others. I steer clear of companies in the technology sector, as there is fierce competition, a war on the price of products, and consequently, it all results in a bloodbath for many companies in that sector.

If you want advice, stay away from the financial services sector too, i.e. invest in banks, for example. In a world ruled mostly by speculators, investing in banking would mean giving your money to people who buy and sell hot air, and if that goes well, you make a little money, but if it goes wrong, you lose a lot of money. I don't know about you, but I don't feel comfortable entrusting my money to someone who buys and sells numbers on a screen. It would be pure and simple speculation.

Another sector that would be advise against is passing fashions, which was born as a fashion that has a crazy "boom" in a short time, and after a year, no one remembers it anymore. Let's take the example of social networks. Let's assume the most famous of all, Facebook, which makes lots of money thanks to companies and individuals' advertising services. I am convinced that the shares' value will continue to rise (as long as it continues to make the right considerations without sending everything to the air with wrong administrative decisions). Still, if one day, a new social network arrives from Asia, everyone is crazy. The typical stupid belief is born that if you are not on that social network, you are nobody, then you risk that the Facebook giant collapses slowly, piece by piece.

So, which sectors to invest in? The ones that first jump into my mind that I would most like to advise you are: transport (everyone will always need to move), communications (everyone will ever need to communicate), tourism (people will continue to travel), commerce, materials, metals (trade, materials and metals have been part of the economic system among populations for years) aerospace and defense (governments invest billions in the development of new technologies and security), agriculture (it too has been part of our world for millennia now), pharmaceutical (I don't think there is any need to tell you how much humans spend on pharmaceutical treatments), mining (for example companies that mine diamonds or gold.

LAW NO. 6: CHOOSE A MAXIMUM OF 10 TITLES.

Let's be transparent if they are 11 or 12, then it's okay but watch out for more. Many beginners think that having 30 or 40 stocks in their portfolios is the right way to build a healthy equity portfolio, believing that by "spreading" their savings across multiple companies, they will be more likely to find the right companies. Unfortunately, I have bad news for these madmen. There are not a lot of REALLY healthy competitive and performing companies, so going to buy right and left as many shares as possible in the hope of finding the right ones will not make them a good deal, as if out of the 30 companies whose shares they bought, 25 go wrong and, (let's say they were lucky enough to catch those five that go awry. However, they would never be able to compensate for the losses of those 25 that are doing poorly. Furthermore, having 30 or more securities in their portfolio will not guarantee them excellent earnings because of having "spread" their funds in so many (unhealthy) companies. They won't have the option to enter "weighty" (for example they won't have the option to purchase a lot more offers) on organizations solid, which will ensure phenomenal outcomes as opposed to purchasing a couple of portions of numerous uncompetitive organizations.

LAW NO. 7: THINK LONG-TERM

Badly, we live in a society where everyone wants to make money quickly, worry-free, automatically, and above all, very quickly. As for the "very fast," to tell you the truth, there are markets that allow certain things since they give you the possibility to enter the market "on leverage." The only small problem is getting into leverage will enable you to earn quickly and lose a lot just as fast. The difficulty is not to achieve but to accumulate in the long term; it is full of "aspiring traders" who earn and are positive in a short time. But we have to see if their account is complimentary even after 5/10 years because it is useless that they make profits for 1 or 2 years if then the third year they lose everything. These people fall into the category of "speculators," and I can assure you that they have no way out in the long run.

On the other hand, the Professional Investor looks at his long-term investments because this is what matters, accumulating wealth continuously without risking losing them from one year to the next.

WHAT CATEGORY OF TRAINING IS REQUIRED TO BECOME A STOCKBROKER?

Many stockbrokers prefer to employ other beginner stockbrokers who have at least a bachelor's degree, preferably in business administration. Many colleges offer degrees in the business organization, and seeking a degree with accentuation or focus on money can be the proper groundwork for a profession as a stockbroker.

Students of stockbrokers in finance programs take general education courses in English, mathematics and science, and core courses in business administration and economics, accounting, legal issues in business, marketing, management, organizational behavior and systems information.

Then stockbrokers take courses related to their concentration; these courses can cover business capital management, venture and portfolio the board, money related demonstrating, hazard the executives, monetary business sectors and establishments, and corporate account.

Some students do internships with agents' stock exchange while completing his degree. Completing training can give students valuable experience to determine their career path and make them more attractive as candidates for jobs after graduation. Graduates of undergraduate business programs can seek work at brokerage houses.

Most stockbrokers offer new hires on-the-job training that can last several months. During the training, new stockbrokers learn about the financial markets and the products that their brokerage agency sells. They also learn sales methods and prepare to obtain the licenses they need to work legally as a stockbroker. After the training period is over, brokers are expected to build their customer base and start meeting sales quotas.

Are There Any Certification or Licensing Requirements to Be A Stockbroker?

The brokers must have specific securities licenses to buy and sell shares. The Financial Industry Regulatory Authority (FINRA) inspects the registration and licensing of stockbrokers. To register as a representative of your Broker, brokers must pass specific exams administered by FINRA

As stockbrokers, they are required to pass examinations first Series 7 and Series 63. Every sequential test permit agent to play out specific capacities for their Broker, and intermediaries may lead extra tests to show their ability in one sort of speculation or money related assistance.

What Is the Time Frame to Be A Stockbroker?

The brokers can hire brokers stock market directly after

graduating with a bachelor's degree, which typically takes four years to complete. Some earn a Master of Business Administration (MBA) before practicing as stockbrokers. Obtaining an MBA can take an additional two to three years.

How Much Does A Stockbroker Make?

The Bureau of Labor Statistics bunches stockbrokers with different protections, items, and budgetary administrations deals operators. The average annual payment for this group was $ us—71,720 in 2012. The bottom ten percent of the group earned less than $ us. 32,030 that year, while the first ten percent earned more than $ the US. 187,200.

Early in their careers of being a stockbroker, trainees and new stockbrokers earn a salary. Still, as they gain experience, more of their compensation comes from the commission on the sales they complete.

What Are the Job Prospects for Being A Stockbroker?

The Bureau of Labor Statistics expands that crafted by insurances, things and budgetary organizations bargains administrators will create 11 percent somewhere in the range of 2012 and 2020, nearly as quick as the normal development for all occupations. The BLS predicts that stockbrokers who work in products will have the best occupation prospects, yet competition for a wide scope of stockbroker positions will be furious because of the potential for significant compensation. The stockbrokers who have graduate degrees or advanced certification should have the best opportunities to get a job.

What Are the Long-Term Career Prospects for Stockbrokers?

The brokers that provide large amounts of sales may

advance to positions that allow them to interact with larger customers. A stockbroker can start working with individual clients, for example, and then working with small businesses and larger corporations. Some stockbrokers advance to positions of the portfolio manager, and some stockbrokers very successful are offered brokerage companies in their stock market.

How Can I Encounter A Job as A Stockbroker?

Many stockbrokers accumulate their first job offer through associating. Completing an internship while in college is an excellent way to network in the industry, and your work can lead to a job offer after graduation. Even if you don't, the people you meet can be a good source of information about job openings in the future.

If you went to business school, your alumni network could be another right way to connect with people. As you connect with more investment workers, you should learn more about potential job opportunities.

How Can I Learn More About Being A Stockbroker?

You can study turning into a stockbroker by perusing distributions that emphasize Wall Street and business. Websites and publications such as Forbes, the Wall Street Journal, and Investopedia can be good sources of information about financial markets and careers in this field.

Do you have a good head for figures? Do you dream of working in the world of finance a la Gordon Gekko, but without the villainy, then you could become a stockbroker Your job would be to buy and sell financial products like stocks and shares to get the best rewards for customers, whether they are individuals or large corporations.

There are three different types of broker-dealers: discretionary investment management and client decision-making; advisory gives advice, and execution not to provide advice but to carry out the clients' purchase and sale requests.

RESPONSIBILITIES OF A BROKER IN THE STOCK MARKET

- Keeping up with the financial markets
- Research potential strategies for clients
- Regularly review systems to ensure peak performance
- Contact investment analysts to learn more about potential markets
- Transmission of instructions to operators on market prices

WHAT WORK DOES IT TAKE TO BE A STOCKBROKER?

Stockbroker position description:

Buy and sell financial products, such as stocks, bonds, and commodities. Clients can be both organizations and individuals for whom you manage financial products. It can be advisory, discretionary, or functional. Days can be long, now and again over 12 hours, including work snacks, and start hours before the stock exchanges open. Work can be distressing as it includes a lot of cash, significant levels of duty, and time-touchy choices that should be all around determined yet in addition fast.

A stockbroker buys and sells financial products intending to maximize his clients' profit from the transaction. Clients of stockbrokers can be individuals or organizations seeking the greatest profit for their speculations. Your occupation can be an admonition, giving your clients proposals on which money related items would be the most productive or most secure. Optional permits you to deal with a customer's ventures self-rulingly, or an official who might see you purchasing and selling monetary items.

You can decide to feature your work involvement with one of the three claims to fame; paying little mind to the way you pick, filling in as a stockbroker will include: looking at and dealing with customers' speculation portfolios, building up a venture plan with the customer, directing investigations of the market, contact customers and advise them about the exhibition regarding their portfolios and attempt to arrive at new likely customers.

As ought to be self-evident, a stockbroker must wear

different covers, so if you are the person who struggles managing various mental turns for the duration of the day, it may not be the best profession way for you.

SPECIFICATIONS TO BE A STOCKBROKER

Step by step instructions to enter the business:

- o Enroll in an entry level position or stock financier program that organizations offer
- o A horizontal move from another situation inside the money related industry

Vital character characteristics:

Capacity to work under monstrous tension

Speedy investigating

An inclination for math and information

Profoundly created correspondence and relational abilities

Moral honesty and constancy, as the occupation regularly includes moving enormous amounts of cash. Obviously, every business may have different essentials for their up-and-comers.

On the off chance that you are starting at now in the cash related field, you might have the option to progress to the region with insignificant preparing or be picked by businesses for your experience.

In any case, on the grounds that the money related market is a legislature directed industry, you should apply for the appraisals given by the Financial Conduct Authority.

The Authority offers an expansive once-over of capabilities that you will require contingent upon the field in which you wish to practice and the prerequisites that your boss may have:

- CFOA Society UK Level 4 Certificate in Financing Administration
- CISI Level 4 Diploma in Investment Consultative
- CISI Level 7 Master of Affluence Management

Gains - Advantages

Short-length Advantages for a broker

- High money related increases in any event, for experts beginning their expert vocation
- Movement limit inside industry and organizations
- The advancement of an arrangement of customers dependent on their specialization that you convey between organizations is likewise founded on your organization's strategy.

Long-Length Advantages for a Broker

- Greater budgetary security
- High roof for professional success and life span
- Possibility to take a shot at your own or as a counselor, dispensing with high-hazard trades and business pressure.
- Of course, on the off chance that you have the blessing and ability, being a stockbroker can be an incredibly long vocation, with generous monetary profits.
- Most financial organizations promote from within, allowing for great potential for professional development.
- Starting salaries of stockbrokers are usually between 20,000- and 30,000-pounds sterling a year, but there is the possibility that individuals can earn much more.

- Although at first, it will be a battle that includes long work hours, end of the week work, and managing requesting customers, following 5 to 10 years of involvement, you will control your work process and select the client you need to work with.
- When you start, the cash you procure on normal can be as low as 1%.
- This implies that you could have £ 10,000,000 in resources, and with a 30% commission, you would in any case procure just £ 30,0000, £ 40,000. In any case, as your customer base develops and develops, the measure of pay you can create will increment dramatically.
- For model, on the off chance that you procure even 5% on $ 10,000,000 us with a 30% commission, you are considering making $ 150,000 for us a year.
- The normal day for another stockbroker would incorporate seeming two hours before the 6 am market opens to do the important exploration; when the business sectors open, the representative will contact their customers to suggest buys or deals.
- After a very short lunch, which might possibly include meeting likely customers, the last portion of the day is commonly spent gathering customers, finding new customers, and doing desk work.
- Finally, most new specialists spend their eleven and twelve hours cold, calling likely customers, or participating in different exercises to discover new customers.
- Many even decide to deal with Saturdays; on the off chance that you need to encounter what exchanging can resemble, attempt one of the numerous virtual brokers accessible on the web, abundance the executives, resource the board, and private banking.

TYPES OF ADVISORY POSITIONS FOR A STOCKBROKER

1. Personal Banking: Advising middle-income individuals.
2. Privileged Banking: Advice to mid-level clients.
3. Private Banking: Advising high net worth (HNW) or very high net worth individuals on their investments.

This fragment of the monetary business, otherwise called private banking or resource the executives, is basic to affluent people.

Regularly, entering this portion requires a broad organization of amazingly affluent people who trust their judgment and budgetary ability. As a resource supervisor or abundance chief, you won't just be accountable for cash the executives, however you will likewise be arranging your ventures for future development. The calling can be debilitating and unpredictable on the off chance that you expect to enter it straightforwardly.

Commonly, you will begin as an individual financier, which will encourage individuals on the most proficient method to begin contributing. Nonetheless, this is certifiably not an immediate way to abundance the executives. It is an astounding method to get comfortable with contributing exhortation. On the off chance that you are exceptional at your particular employment, you may build up a little arrangement of customers; in the long run, on the off chance that you figure out how to progress through close to home banking, you will work in Privileged Banking.

NEXT DEGREE OF BANKING

This is the following degree of banking and normally

manages lower esteem clients than private banking, yet has fundamentally the same as duties and errands. Many insider banking advisers remain in the industry because private banking's transition can lose clients and, ultimately, revenue. The beneficial thing about arriving at the higher classes of private banking is that the way of life gets much simpler, yet that is presumably a result of every one of those 16-hour shifts you had from the get-go in your profession.

Frequently, when a stockbroker picks up experience working in the business sectors, they can progress to a profession in abundance the executives. This requires a demonstrated history. An abundance supervisor's vital capacity is to administer all individuals' money related exercises, including retirement, actual resources, market resources, and income.

Despite the fact that they are paid richly to provoke their clients, it is easy to make wrong decisions that cost you a customer or, more awful, the entirety of your clients because of an absence of confidence and faith in you; high salaries often carry high risks.

FIVE TIPS TO LEARN TO FUND INTO THE STOCK MARKET FOR BEGINNERS

It is amazing the number of individuals need to figure out how to contribute however don't set out to do as such for different reasons. It is additionally predominant to meet individuals who are urged to venture out wind up leaving it without accomplishing their objective. It is a way that requires some investment; it tends to be testing, yet it is productive, and it is justified, despite any trouble. With these five hints for figuring out how to put resources into the securities exchange, I need to assist amateurs with beginning this way effectively without simply trying.

1. **Master to Invest from The Best:**

    It is basic to realize how to isolate the grain from the refuse. The media, particularly the Internet, are brimming with counterfeit speculation masters who offer idiot-proof approaches to put assets into the financial exchange and make enormous money in a short time. Most, if not all, are scoundrels who procure their living by selling pointless books and courses at extravagant costs.

    To know who the best is, we must turn to the recorded benefit of their speculations. Warren Buffett, Peter Lynch, David Einhorn, Phillip Fisher, the administrators of Best contribute. They have all acquired incredible profits for their ventures, causing numerous investors and members of their assets rich who to have confided in them as long as possible. You can procure a great deal in a year on the off chance that you are fortunate, however a financial specialist's worth is demonstrated over the long haul.

    What do the vast majority of the best financial specialists share practically speaking? Who puts resources into long haul stocks following the way of thinking of significant worth contributing? They don't exchange intraday, break down graphs, or put resources into exceptionally utilized subsidiaries. Try not to sell the cruiser with bogus guarantees; on the off chance that you need to figure out how to contribute like the best, you should zero in on esteem contributing.

2. **Read A Lot and Of Quality:**

When we are evident that we will gain from the best, that we will figure out how to contribute as indicated by the essentials of significant worth contributing, we should get down to work. To do this, the most ideal route is to peruse a great deal. In any case, that isn't adequate; we should search for quality substance. There are three essential wellsprings of substance that we ought not preclude:

Books: The Basic Source of Wisdom. I generally suggest starting with " The Intelligent Investor " by Benjamin Graham, where worth contributing basics are set up, instructing us to think like a business visionary speculator. As the quantity of venture books is tremendous, I suggest that you experience my part of " prescribed books to figure out how to put resources into the financial exchange, "which will without a doubt be of incredible use to you.

Interpersonal organizations for speculators: This are wellsprings of data that we can't preclude by the same token. To discover which informal communities to utilize, I suggest you investigate my article on the three interpersonal organizations for financial specialists that merit being on.

3. **Be Patient:**

Prior to beginning, you need to realize that figuring out how to contribute requires significant investment, quite a while. Also, contributing is a craftsmanship that requires constant discovering that endures forever. The specialty of reversal has an expectation to absorb information fundamentally the same as that of military craftsmanship. You can ace the basics in a brief timeframe, yet it takes a lifetime to be a devoted instructor, and the learning cycle never closes.

4. **Apply the Theory:**

    Having a strong hypothetical base is basic to figure out how to contribute. In any case, the training can't be saved. It is important to make up for scholastic learning with reasonable ones. For instance, you can begin by taking a gander at the introductions of results and yearly records of some recorded organizations to become accustomed to it over the long run. It isn't hard to dissect the organizations top to bottom later on.

5. **Be Consistent:**

    In figuring out how to put resources into the securities exchange, similarly as with eats less, actual exercise, or studies, persistence is fundamental. As the Roman writer Ovid stated: "The drop of water punctures the stone not in light of its quality, but since of its steadiness."

    My suggestion is to build up a guide with explicit targets. For instance, dissect an organization consistently or read a book like clockwork. Interestingly, these destinations are exact, sensible, and adjusted to our time and information.

THE WORLD OF CRYPTOCURRENCIES

The cryptocurrency or cryptocurrency is a digital currency that uses cryptography to provide a secure payment system. These encryption techniques serve to regulate the generation of monetary units and verify the transfer of funds. They do not need a central bank or other institution to control them.

Cryptocurrency, likewise called virtual cash or cryptographic money, is computerized cash. That implies there are no actual coins or bills - everything is on the web. You can move cryptographic money to somebody on the Internet without a go-between, for example, a bank. The most mainstream cryptographic types of cash are Bitcoin and Ether. However, new digital currencies keep on being made.

Individuals could utilize cryptocurrencies to make speedy installments and to keep away from exchange expenses. A few people may gain digital money as a venture, trusting that it will increment in esteem. Cryptocurrencies can be purchased with a Visa or, at times, through a cycle called " mining." Cryptocurrencies are stored in a wallet or digital wallet, either online, on your computer, or another physical medium. Before buying a cryptocurrency, you have to know that it does not have the same protections as when using US dollars. You also have to know that scammers ask people to pay you with a cryptocurrency because they know that those payments are usually irreversible.

Cryptocurrencies are an assortment of advanced cash, which are those that don't live in an actual structure, however that fills in as a trade money, permitting moment exchanges through the Internet and paying little mind to fringes. Other advanced cash types are virtual monetary forms (normally constrained by designers), electronic cash, and Internet coupons. The main digital currency to begin working was Bitcoin in 2009, and from that point forward, others with various qualities have showed up, for example, Litecoin, Ethereum, Bitcoin Cash, Ripple, Dogecoin.

GENESIS OF CRYPTOCURRENCY

In 1983, American cryptographer David Chaum imagined an electronic cash cryptographic framework called eCash. Afterward, in 1995, it actualized DigiCash, which utilized cryptography to deliver cash exchanges mysterious, but with unified issuance and repayment (installment). This framework expected programming to pull out cash from a bank and assign explicit encryption keys prior to sending it to a beneficiary. This allowed the serious cash to be untraceable by the dependable bank, the assembly, or any untouchable.

In 1996, the NSA distributed an examination named How to Make a Mint: The Cryptography of Anonymous Electronic Cash. This exploration portrayed a digital currency framework posted on a MIT 10 mailing list. Later in 1997, it was created in The American Law Review (Vol. 46, Issue 4).

Wei Dai first portrayed the idea or thought of digital currency in 1998, where he proposed making another sort of scattered cash that would utilize cryptography as a methods for control. At the same time, the main digital currency made was Bitcoin, underlying 2009 by alias Satoshi Nakamoto, which utilizes the SHA-2 arrangement of cryptographic capacities (precisely SHA-256) as its PoW (evidence of work) plot. Consequently, there have been different criptomonedas, as Name coin (an endeavor to decentralize the arrangement of area names DNS, which would make web oversight troublesome), Litecoin (which utilizes scrypt as a PoW conspire, just as for quicker exchange affirmation), Peercoin (which utilizes a mixture PoW/PoS plot [test of work/evidence of stake], likewise has an expansion pace of around 1%) and Freicoin (which executed Silvio Gesell's idea adding devaluation over the long run). Numerous different digital currencies have been made, despite the fact that not all have been fruitful, particularly those that have not brought any development.

Since its commencement, digital forms of money have steadily picked up the consideration of the overall population and the media. Since 2011, interest has risen quickly, particularly during Bitcoin's soaring ascent in April 2013. The stop criptomonedas market is extended to reach $ 2.1 trillion of every 2018.

On August 6, 2014, the U.K. reported that it authorized an investigation of digital forms of money from the Treasury. This examination should show what job this sort of cash could play in the U.K. economy. It likewise dispatched what guidelines ought to be thought of.

TYPES OF CRYPTOCURRENCIES

Although traditional money, whether in the form of currency or paper, is still the most widely used method for exchanging goods and services between users, the truth is that cryptocurrencies are becoming a better alternative to carry out these operations. In this sense, it should be known that Bitcoin was the pioneer in this entire process; however, currently, there are many others with which you can make the transactions you want. **Here some of the cryptocurrencies most used by users currently on the market:**

Bitcoin

How could it be otherwise? Bitcoin is the cryptocurrency that occupies the first place on our list. It is logical considering that it was the pioneer when creating a virtual monetary system. Bitcoin was presented in 2009 as the first digital currency in history, and for this reason, it is still the most used by users. Bitcoin is mainly used as a way of exchanging through the network. All payments made with this virtual currency are anonymous, and the codes used for transactions are unreadable. Hence the system is entirely secure.

In recent years, it has experienced remarkable growth, reaching a value of almost 1,000 times. Each unit can currently range between $ 400 and $ 500, although it reached $ 1,000 at one point, thanks to the multiple transactions that users around the world had made.

Litecoin

Second, we find Litecoin. This cryptocurrency is located in the second position because it is considered the best alternative to Bitcoin. This cryptocurrency uses the same algorithm as the previous one, and also the process to use it is practically the same. The vital contract between Litecoin and Bitcoin is that the former has a much lower value, ranging from $ 2 to $ 3.

One of the significant advantages that Litecoin offers is that it allows us to make payments immediately at a low cost, almost close to zero. This cryptocurrency has been in operation in the market since October 2011.

Primecoin

Another cryptocurrency that is widely used in the market is Primecoin. Unlike the previous two, in this case, the system is established from the prime numbers. The correlation of these numbers is forming chains of figures, which is called Cunningham.

Also, with Primecoin, all the transactions carried out will be done much faster than with Bitcoin. Some surpass a speed of up to 8 or multiple times more than the first. Perhaps, the only drawback that Primecoin has is that it has a low value in the market, touching $ 0.03 per unit.

Namecoin

Namecoin is presented as one of the few cryptocurrencies that are not commercial; instead, it is used to create web page addresses. The advantage is that all these portals are free and independent, so they are not controlled by the relevant bodies that regulate the Internet.

Once you create the addresses, they are typically sold to users who are interested in purchasing them. The utilization of

Namecoin is useful as drawn-out speculation, even though the estimation of every unit in the market isn't excessively high, being 0.5 dollars. Even though it has an alternate capacity, this cryptocurrency additionally utilizes similar boundaries as the Bitcoin framework.

Ripple

If it is said that Litecoin was the best alternative to Bitcoin, it is affirmed that Ripple is the second most feasible option. This cryptocurrency operation is very similar to that of the first since all the transactions carried out are real-time and relatively fast.

Ripple's advantage is that it has its currency exchange system. With this cryptocurrency, we can acquire practically any product we want, entirely only and without the need to purchase other programs.

Dogecoin

Although most cryptocurrencies are based on the Bitcoin algorithm, this time, the reference system for this cryptocurrency is Litecoin. What happens is that it includes other characteristics that make it unique.

The maximum benefit that we can obtain using Dogecoin is that its system can generate blocks much faster, almost one per minute. For this reason, it is capable of carrying out around 40,000 transactions daily.

Dogecoin became very popular in 2014, and one of its

most significant functions is that it is used to make contributions to NGOs and other non-profit organizations. Currently, its market value is around $ 0.00015 per unit.

Ethereum

When talking about Ethereum, it's referred to the program by which the system of a specific type of cryptocurrency is governed. But the virtual currency in question is baptized as Ether. At first, this system hit the market as an update of the primitive Bitcoin, including many improvements in this first system's programming, mainly in terms of the programming language, which already had certain limitations.

Through Ethereum, many transactions can be carried out, and alternative applications have even been created to continue improving the system today. Today, the maximum number of Ether that can be issued per year cannot exceed 18 million.

Dash

It is one of the most recent systems that has undergone numerous modifications in recent years. It is about the freest cryptocurrencies that exist today since all the transactions made with them are public, and they are also within a completely independent context. Being a fully decentralized system, Dash is always in continuous transformation, creating updates from time to time to offer the most renewed and innovative services to users.

The value of Dash today usually ranges between 20 and 23 dollars, although it exceeded this threshold at the beginning of 2017, reaching almost 24 dollars per unit. The most significant difference that Dash has concerning other systems is that to invest with this cryptocurrency and be part of the system itself; you have to add a minimum amount of 1,000 Dash.

THE MAIN CHARACTERISTICS OF CRYPTOCURRENCIES

- **Decentralization**: there is no central entity that controls or regulates its operation. Just as traditional currencies all have a Central Bank in charge of determining aspects such as their impression (which can directly impact their value), their price is determined by the market itself in the case of cryptocurrencies.

- **High volatility:** in line with the previous point, the absence of a central entity that regulates their operation makes them a target for speculators who seek a short-term profit through more aggressive investments. Through capital movements, large investors can make the value of a cryptocurrency vary without there being, behind this change, a justification or correlation on its real situation.

- **They are found on platforms that allow operations without intermediaries:** this is one of the main aspects that represents an advance compared to what currently exists. Blockchain platforms will enable the signing an agreement of smart contracts, a fact that considerably reduces costs since the figure of the intermediary disappears. The verification of transactions occurs through a blockchain system through which the authenticity of the operation is verified.

- **Low costs:** as a consequence of the absence of intermediaries, carrying out transactions on Blockchain platforms through cryptocurrencies implies a low cost compared to traditional ones with other means.

- **Confidentiality:** it is one of the most appreciated and, at the same time, criticized aspects of the crypto universe. On the one hand, it prevents personal data of individuals and transactions from being in the hands of third parties (such as banks). Then again, it is denounced that it could be an approach to launder cash or do unlawful tasks.

- **Development of security systems:** although the platforms where exchanges are made and the wallets where the tokens are kept make essential efforts in terms of security, there have been different hacker attacks that have managed to get hold of high amounts of cryptocurrencies.

- **Personal and non-transferable keys:** to try to ensure that they cannot be stolen, each person is the only one who knows the access keys to their cryptocurrency space. However, there is an obvious risk that, in the event of a loss or neglect of these, it is impossible to access the investment made, which is lost.

- **Possibility of converting them into other currencies:** cryptocurrencies have an equivalence in value with the other fiat currencies that we know. On the other hand, it is condemned that it very well may be a way to deal with wash money or do unlawful errands.

- **Possibility of purchasing and selling activities:** the future achievement of cryptographic forms of money will be resolved, to an enormous degree, constantly to-day utilize that individuals make of them. Right now, but there are very few companies concerning the global that accept payments with cryptocurrencies. One of the great unknowns of the future is whether this will go further or, on the contrary, will not progress.

CORRELATIONS BETWEEN CRYPTOCURRENCY AND BROKER

Until now, the cryptocurrency market is filling in size, and the quantity of individuals who are keen on this advanced resource is constantly expanding. There are currently more than 1,000 cryptocurrencies; many can be used as means of electronic payments, others were created to be used only within specific platforms and others to register ownership of a particular asset. Bitcoin, the most famous cryptocurrency, stands out for its security, diffusion and ease of exchange. It is decentralized, so no one rules it. There is no central issuer as in the case of dollars or euros. The bitcoin has a defined issue at the time of its creation and is unchangeable. The production comes from people and companies around the world who dedicate resources to mining.

What is a crypto broker? A crypto broker is a broker that permits you to put resources into Bitcoin and different digital forms of money, for example, Ethereum, Dash, Litecoin, and so on in Forex.

When buying cryptocurrencies, the user can choose to go

to a broker or an exchange, so it is convenient to know the differences between the two so as not to lose money. The broker is an intermediary who owns cryptocurrencies and sells it at a price and commissions it considers. Also, if the user wants to sell his crypto, it is the broker who will set the price he wishes to pay for those coins.

Spread: It is the difference between the buy and sell price that the broker establishes on its platform, and it is its primary collection tool: the higher the spread, the more money you can earn between operations.

Stock: Brokers buy and sell cryptos with their stock, which is limited. Therefore, poor stock management can mean that customers are left without the possibility of trading. Generally, this occurs when there is a strong movement in price or when there is volatility. So, it is not surprising that, mysteriously, in times of significant volatility, they stop working. Also, if they do not have stock of a specific asset, they will delay the crediting of funds from customers interested in buying this missing asset.

Problems with Accreditations: the broker always speculates between the available stock it has, the price at which it buys and the general market price. If you see a trend in the price for which you should wait to credit the balance to the user to obtain more profit, you will do so without any doubt.

Commissions: It is very common to see advertisements that say: "No commissions!", But in these cases, the commissions are attached to the surcharge they charge at the time of buying or the discount they make when selling.

On the other hand, an exchange offers to purchase and sale of crypto with a different scheme. Instead of a broker that manages its stock with what users sell it, in exchanges there are order books, where all concurrent users of the platform load their buy and sell orders, creating among all the availability of crypto, without the need for an intermediary who raises prices.

HOW TO INVEST IN CRYPTOCURRENCIES: WATCH OUT VOLATILITY!

The market is characterized by intense daily volatility, i.e. the price of cryptocurrencies can fluctuate strongly during short periods. In a few hours, the price could rise and fall by up to 10%. The intense volatility is due to the fact that being a developing market, it is not yet clear what the anchor value of these new digital assets could be. The economic theory on which most financial modelling is based dictates the assumption that the price of an asset correlates to the present value of its future cash flows.

In the case of cryptocurrencies, this assessment is challenging to apply and, therefore, there is no oscillation around an equilibrium point as occurs for other assets. Still, the trading price can rise or fall significantly, even for an extended period. Because of this, if you are looking for a low-risk investment, I strongly advise against considering crypto and therefore refer you to articles by colleagues who have dealt with less risky securities.

Suppose also, you are in search of aggressive investment, with all the benefits and risks that derive from it. In that case, the strategies to adopt to invest in cryptocurrency will be describe, as well as the crucial variables to keep in mind.

THE 5 GOLDEN RULES FOR INVESTING IN CRYPTOCURRENCY

Here are the five golden rules for winning investments in the world of cryptocurrencies:

- **1st RULE:**
   Crypto, unlike other currencies, are not tied to the monetary policies of central banks: their price does not have a direct relationship with news and events of a financial nature. So, don't waste time waiting for information from the ECB and the Fed. Above all, keep an eye on the news relating to international regulations on this market. When authorizations or restrictions are enacted, they will strongly impact the price of digital assets. For example, in January 2018, when the Chinese and Korean governments closed some exchange platforms, Bitcoin lost 10%.

- **2nd RULE:**
   Relying on technical analysis indicators. As previously mentioned, the cryptocurrency market is affected by strong instability, and investors rely on less analytical tools than those used for other assets.
   Identifying supports, resistances, and the trend of each cryptocurrency of interest will undoubtedly be important in making your investments profitable in the short term. Unlike other markets, where large investors have cutting-edge tools and models, technical analysis is arguably the most commonly used valuation with crypto.

- **3rd RULE:**
   Interpret the market moods and ride them. At a time when the market has extreme confidence in

a cryptocurrency, or when the majority of investors are convinced about a price rise, the price will continue to rise, and you can earn if you can understand and anticipate the general mood.

- **4th RULE:**

    Diversify your portfolio. The main advice is not to invest all your savings in a single currency, but to create a portfolio with multiple cryptocurrencies to reduce the total risk of the positions. Suppose you have some basic knowledge of statistics. In that case, you could try to calculate the correlation between the cryptocurrencies you prefer and then select those that have a correlation coefficient as far away from 1, even better if negative.

    Two digital currencies are correlated when the trend of their price behaves similarly: if the price of a cryptocurrency goes lower or higher, the cost of the related will tend to act in the same way.

    Assuming that over some time, crypto in your wallet becomes extremely popular and its price rises, you will be able to earn even if the other digital currencies perform poorly. Instead, if the currency goes through a negative period, you will cover the losses with the performance of the rest. This strategy is applied by all large investors to take on lower risks.

- **5th RULE:**

    It is not worth going against the trend. If the price of a cryptocurrency is falling, don't buy it until the value picks up (the so-called "rebound").

HOW ACADEMICS INVEST IN CRYPTO-CURRENCY

Many professional investors have highlighted a strong correlation between the price of cryptocurrencies and their trends on Google to create predictive models that exploit these two indicators.

Google Trends is a useful free tool that allows you to know, for a given the word, the number of searches made on the search engine. Generally, when a person wants to invest in any asset, he starts by doing searches through the appropriate Google tab.

Thanks to this merchandise, you will be able to understand what are the ideas of investors and, therefore, in which direction the price of a currency is going. An idea, for example, would be to type "Bitcoin" to compare the price trend and that of the graph shown, to determine whether to buy or sell the currency mentioned above. You will notice that they move in a very similar way: using this tool, and helping you with the technical analysis indicators, you too can predict the right moment to buy/sell.

STEPS IN FINDING CRYPTOCURRENCY BROKER

Whether you are already clear on which cryptocurrency you want to invest in or only looking to test and build your strategy. keep the following feature in mind to choose the right cryptocurrency broker:

1. **Regulated and secure crypto brokers**

Always check which is the regulatory body that authorizes and controls the broker (all the better if it is located in Europe) and verify that it also maintains the accounts of its clients segregated from its own (in theory it cannot touch the traders' deposits since they do not belong to you). Buying cryptocurrencies is relatively accessible and straightforward to any mortal, but the highest possible security guarantees must be demanded.

2. **Do you already know in which cryptocurrency you are going to invest?**
There are currently hundreds of cryptocurrencies available. However, you cannot trade all of them. Most brokers allow trading with "bigger" cryptocurrencies such as Bitcoin or Ethereum, while lesser-known ones such as Zcash or Monero are tradable through a few brokers.

3. **Cryptocurrency Fees and Spreads**
Check all broker fees before investing; some outstanding brokers do not require maintenance or management fees. The spread that is currently being paid for virtual currencies is highly variable, from 0.0030 for a minor currency (like Ripple) to 25.00 pips min. for Bitcoins (since their price is much higher).

4. **Demo account + Trading platform**
Opening a demo account and practicing is the best decision you can make, whether you have already set an investment strategy or not. You first need to enlighten yourself with the tool and, fundamentally, with cryptocurrency trading. The best brokers offer play money demos with no restrictions.

Also, remember that the trading platform is your workplace and therefore you have to master it and feel comfortable with it. Depending on your style and experience in the world of investment, you will need software with more or fewer functionalities, for P.C. or your Android, etc.

5. **The services of the broker**
It is not only recommended that the broker has good customer service in Spanish, but also offers tools specially designed for trading CFDs, for example, investor trends, copy-trading, signals of Forex, trader statistics, etc.

THE NEWBORN CHINESE DIGITAL YUAN

China has gradually increased testing of its first central bank-backed digital currency. It is known there as DCEP (for "digital currency electronic payment" or electronic payment in digital currency). While different nations have made comparative endeavors to dispatch computerized sovereign money, the steps that the world's second-largest economy takes in this direction are undoubtedly more meaningful.

WHAT IS CHINA'S DIGITAL CURRENCY?

DCEP is a computerized currency supported by the yuan. That sets it aside from Bitcoin and other cryptocurrencies, whose values can vary wildly based on speculation, making them unsuitable for widespread use, in the eyes of most governments. The DCEP, however, must be as stable as the physical yuan.

Like cash, each digital yuan is created, signed, and issued by PBOC. However, unlike money, the bank retains the ability to track the movement of each digital currency it gives. Commercial banks distribute DCEP to their customers, who can download the currency from their bank accounts into digital wallets or apps, similar to withdrawing cash at an ATM.

With a digital wallet full of DCEP, consumers can make instant contactless payments to anyone else using the service, whether it's at the grocery store or paying a friend. In theory, this could eliminate the need for third-party digital payment services such as WeChat or Alipay, currently widely used in China.

This digital currency will be corresponding to the renminbi and can be freely exchanged with the renminbi. More importantly, it is said to be usable without the Internet. But unlike Bitcoin and other existing encrypted digital currencies based on blockchain technology, the central bank may still be the issuer of the currency. Officials of the People's Bank of China stated that the digital currency would adopt a two-tier operating system. The People's Bank will first connect with commercial banks, and the commercial banks will be responsible for connecting with ordinary people.

China's digital currency fully draws on the third-party payment methods of e-commerce companies, and eventually disposed of the improvement thoughts of customary electronic money. It alludes to the outsider instalment arrangement of e-commerce organizations and uses a blockchain system for security verification.

A survey report of the Bank for International Settlements

in 2019 showed that 80% of central banks stated that they set up a central bank digital currency project, and 10% of central banks are ready to release digital currencies within three years. The U.S. Federal Fund and the U.S. Congress strongly oppose the implementation of digital currencies by U.S. e-commerce companies, fearing that digital currencies will shake the domination of the U.S. dollar currency. Nonetheless, on August 13, 2020, the top managerial staff of the U.S. Federal Reserve revealed at a meeting held in the San Francisco area of the U.S. Federal Reserve that the U.S. Federal Reserve has begun testing a digital currency.

As introductory as 2014, the People's Bank of China set up an advanced cash research venture. In 2016, the People's Bank of China Digital Currency Research Institute was set up and begun to create Chinese advanced cash.

Chinese advanced currency isn't just unique in relation to electronic cash yet in addition, not quite the same as the money created by the Federal Reserve Board of the United States. China's computerized money is another currency framework dependent on power. China's digital currency fully draws on the third-party payment methods of e-commerce companies, and at last disposed of the advancement thoughts of conventional electronic cash. It alludes to the outsider instalment arrangement of web-based business organizations and embraces the blockchain framework in terms of security verification—a digital currency with unique Chinese characteristics.

ORIGIN OF THE DCEP

The beginning of the development of DCEP can be traced back to 2014. It was around then, in which the PboC proposed making advanced money. The bank's then-director, Zhou

Xiaochuan, pioneered the concept and established the World's first official institution for the research and advancement of legal digital currency: The Central Bank's Digital Currency Institute.

The goal of this examination bunch was to improve the Chinese yuan framework with blockchain innovation. This, while China was already beginning to apply harsh sanctions against Bitcoin and free cryptocurrencies. Sanctions that remain active today in that nation. China embraced blockchain technology but trying to maintain the control that cryptocurrencies take away from it. As we explained in the article on CBDC, Bitcoin and a CBDC are radically different things: while Bitcoin gives freedom to the citizen, a CBDC enslaves.

However, despite the establishment of this research and development group, progress in this regard was limited. It was not until 2017, with the official establishment of the group in Beijing, that China began to take rapid steps in the construction of its digital currency. Among the primary responsibilities of this team was to focus on innovation and development of digital currency and financial technology. In addition to carrying out research and legal effect of digital currency. All this in accordance with the national strategic deployment and the central bank's general working agreement.

DCEP's advancement steps were additionally quickened when, in 2019, Facebook declared the dispatch of Libra, its private computerized cash. This situation put China on alert since, in its opinion, Libra would endanger not only its economy but also its site of economic and financial innovation with a digital currency of global reach. To this was also added the fact that the Libra Association was a clear rejection of the digital economic system that China seeks to create with DCEP. All of this prompted the nation to accelerate its plans to launch DCEP.

Subsequently, at long last, following a couple of long stretches of advancement, it was declared on June 22, 2020, that China had just finished the DCEP back-end framework. In any case, China is still in pilot testing as a feature of the innovative work measure. At long last, it has been declared that other Chinese urban communities, unfamiliar organizations and scenes for the 2022 Winter Olympics facilitated by China, will partake in the DCEP tests. This clarifies that China as of now has all it requires to begin its undertaking set up.

OBJECTIVES OF THE DCEP

With DCEP, China seeks to create the first digital currency supported by one of the World's significant economies. The objective is to link 1: 1 its current fiat mass that currently uses the Renminbi (RMB), for a digital currency that any citizen can use to pay for products and services in the nation. At the same time, DCEP seeks to increase its circulation and turn this currency into a currency with a greater international scope. A strategy that aims to turn the Chinese money into the direct opponent of the Dollar.

Although saying it sounds easier than making it a reality. One of the significant problems of China in its plan is the enormous control that the State exercises over its economy, the constant devaluation of the currency. The little transparency and the lack of investment guarantees in the nation, whose regulators always seek to have significant participation in companies that are established within the territory. The situation is beginning to blur rapidly at a time when China starts to exert more substantial pressure on economic poles such as Hong Kong, and relations with Taiwan and Japan begin to strain.

Along with this, we have that China has not been incredibly open with companies from the crypto world. On the one hand, recently talking about Bitcoin or naming it was a risk that few dared to take, and today. However, the risk is lower; few are those who dare to speak freely about Bitcoin and cryptocurrencies, or about how China's digital currency and CBDCs are an absolute contradiction to the philosophy with which Blockchain was born.

However, the current global outlook suggests that stable coins and CBDCs will continue to grow and take on critical economic spaces around the World. And in that sense, China does not want to stay away from the geopolitical, geoeconomic, geocommercial game and global influences. In that sense, China's commitment to DCEP remains clear: "the DCEP is a CBDC, and we must make our nation and the world adopt it." Mostly when it is known that only 1.6% of global international reserves are protected in Yuan, leaving China far behind in international currency trade.

If these goals are achieved, the DCEP will occupy an important place within the status quo of international currencies, which will undoubtedly contribute to Chinese trade. A risky economic and technological bet that could begin to pay off by 2022. Especially considering the massive group of users that DCEP could have, which is estimated at more than 1.6 billion users. And the reason is that systems like Apple Pay China, AliPay, WeChat, and other digital payment systems will be closely tied to this digital currency.

THE TECHNOLOGY BEHIND THE DCEP HOW DOES THE CHINESE DIGITAL CURRENCY WORK?

The creation of the DCEP is closely linked to blockchain technology; in fact, its operation as such is possible thanks to this technology. From the data that is known, the Central Bank of the Chinese People (PboC) has under its control, the central nodes of the network. At the same time, a series of allied banks and private companies will be able to operate complementary nodes to support the power of the system.

Information about the consensus protocol, mining algorithm, block generation, and the cryptography used is still a state secret. Nobody is aware of these details, and doubtfully they will be known in the near future knowing how jealous China is regarding its national technologies.

What we do know and have made public is that DCEP will be a centralized digital currency, controlled by the PboC. In addition, the coin will have a distribution system divided into two stages. Something similar to all CBDCs.

This system is designed so that the PboC can maintain control, but at the same time, large national companies and banks can play an essential role in its operation. A certain level of the task and power distribution, which seeks to keep the system running smoothly, especially in terms of scalability, since the network plans to serve at least 1.6 billion users globally continuously.

Among the organizations and banks that are behind this activity are monsters, for example, AliPay, WeChat, Union Pay, Huawei, Tencent, Ant Financial, Bank of China, Agricultural Bank of China, Construction Bank of China, the Industrial and monetary Bank of China and other people who will undoubtedly join this giant.

Another important point about the technology and operation of DCEP is given by its level of privacy and anonymity, two characteristics that cash has today. Well, in this sense, the PboC has clarified that DCEP will have controlled confidentiality and anonymity, making it clear that the authorities will be able to know everything about the economic movements of individuals if they wish, but that the public will not have access to these functions.

In addition to this, the PboC can have live access to each and every one of the DCEP wallets that have been created, whether they are in China or anywhere in the World. In short, as in the rest of CBDC, you will never own your money, and they can take your money from you if a central entity deems it convenient.

LEGALITY IN CHINA AND THE REST OF THE WORLD

At this particular point, you will have already seen that DCEP may be a blockchain-powered digital currency. However, its principles are light years away from the spirit of coins like Bitcoin. To that, you can add that the use of DCEP both in China and in the rest of the World is tied to Chinese law. This means that Chinese law will take precedence over any other local or international law for cases of control and access to your financial history and management of wallets.

To lay it more out plainly, we should take the expressions of Huang Qifan, leader of the China International Economic

Exchange Center, who said that they have been chipping away at DCEP for five to six years and is completely certain that it very well may be presented as the money related framework from the nation. Also, Qifan remarked on the accompanying in the China Finance Forum: "DCEP can accomplish the constant assortment of information identified with the creation and utilization of the cash, giving helpful data to the arrangement of cash and the use of money related approaches".

In short, European laws like the GPDR or other laws that protect bank secrecy, economic and financial privacy do not exist for the DCEP. In China, this will have a well-crafted legal framework that will serve to control this vast global financial and economic intelligence machine. But in the remainder of the World, it will indeed not be allowed because of the apparent danger it represents.

CHINA AND THE NEED FOR A DIGITAL CURRENCY FOR ITS NATION

China's need for the launch of the DCEP is drawn from its need to consolidate its economic presence and global influence. Converting DCEP into a highly liquid global currency seeks to boost its use as a reserve currency. In addition to project their companies as financial giants for the provision of services at a worldwide level. All these actions seek to dethrone the dollar as the global reference currency. And they even put the euro as the common currency of Europe at risk.

The reason? DCEP could offer better mechanisms for cross-border payments at a lower cost. In addition to providing greater "security" and above all, more incredible speed, characteristics that exceed the current international payment system. Hence, systems like SWIFT and SEPA actively seek to develop payment systems that are cheaper and faster than their current options. This is work that is already beginning to bring its results.

However, China has a formidable opponent, as SWIFT is the World's most widely used bank transfer mechanism. The SWIFT network, which began operations in 1973, enables financial institutions around the world to send and get economic exchanges in a protected, normalized and dependable way, although not as fast as current times demand.

And while China has the CIPS (China International Payment System) for banks, the creation of the DCEP will put this system aside for one that is faster, more easily adaptable and has a global reach. Quite merely, DCEP is a better development option, and hence China is betting everything on this development today. Moreover, in the midst of a frontal confrontation between China and the United States that has resulted in several events of the trade war in recent years.

Given these events, China's need for a digital currency like DCEP is evident. It is not only a currency for your nation but a vehicle of economic domination. One that he urgently needs to be able to continue with his plans to establish himself as the World's first superpower by dethroning the United States. Hence, many media, especially Chinese press, see the DCEP as the "third wave" targeting the United States.

CHARACTERISTICS OF CHINA'S DIGITAL CURRENCY

China's digital currency has the following characteristics:

1. It is entirely free of dependence on the existing Internet or the "Internet", and digital currency settlement can be carried out even when there is no network. This makes China's digital currency and electronic currency and existing third-party payment systems have a fundamental difference. That is to say; consumers only need to carry mobile terminal equipment and store digital currency in the mobile terminal equipment. Then, there is no need for the Internet to connect the portable terminal equipment to realize currency settlement directly. In this way, it can get rid of the Internet and avoid the threat of digital currency transactions due to security loopholes in the information transmission of the Internet. At the same time, funds can be settled at any time with the help of widely used mobile terminal equipment.

2. The security of China's digital currency is based on the sovereign currency management system. The digital currency issued by China does not establish a central information transmission system, and all transaction information is transmitted to the central system but uses a distributed security protection system, which is commonly understood by people as a blockchain system. If the digital currency transaction is not authenticated by other information, then the digital currency transaction cannot be included in the design, it will not be recognized, and the transaction cannot be completed. Therefore, the widespread promotion of digital currency can combat fraud crimes to a certain extent, and can also reduce corrupt dealings to a certain extent.

3. The issuance of digital currency can significantly save transaction costs and currency management costs. As we

all know, in the field of currency issuance and circulation, there is a phenomenon that "the power is one foot high and the evil one is high". To ensure that the currency issued by each country will not be counterfeited, many technical elements are often added. The application of new materials and technologies objectively leads to a substantial increase in currency printing costs. To solve this problem, issuing digital currency is undoubtedly the best choice.

On the surface, digital currency is a set of numbers, but behind the digital currency, there is strong technical support. Based on the computerized money test directed by the People's Bank of China, China's advanced cash issues computerized money dependent on the expansion of sovereign credit and business credit. In layman's terms, China's computerized cash isn't legitimately given by the People's Bank of China, yet by the People's Bank of China for public business banks. After the business bank acquires the advanced cash gave by the People's Bank of China, it depends on the business bank's credit to give computerized money. In other words, the Chinese digital currency has dual credit attributes.

On the one hand, the People's Bank of China issues currency, which is guaranteed by China's sovereign credit. In different circumstances, the People's Bank of China issues digital currency to commercial banks, and commercial banks use digital currency externally, which is guaranteed by the credit of commercial banks. This gives China's digital currency an unprecedented credit foundation. The issuance of digital currency by a commercial bank means that a particular credit guarantee contract has been signed between the commercial bank and the user. Once a problem occurs, the commercial bank first assumes the guarantee responsibility. Commercial banks can report to the People's Bank of China after taking the guarantee responsibility. The People's Bank of China relies on sovereignty to solve problems. Therefore, no matter where the digital currency issued by China has issues, it will eventually become a sovereignty issue for China. According to the principle of "sovereign immunity", China can safeguard its national sovereignty anywhere and, in any way, and it is not subject to the jurisdiction of judicial organs of other countries. The digital currency distributed by the People's Bank of China is not for every consumer, but for China's state-owned commercial banks. China's state-owned commercial banks have relatively high credit ratings. Therefore, consumers obtain digital currency through state-owned commercial banks, and the risk of using them is relatively low. It can be said that the creditworthiness of the digital currency issued by China is unmatched by the electronic money issued by e-commerce companies in any other country.

4. China's unique digital currency issuance method allows China to bypass the existing international transaction rules in the process of digital currency promotion, opening the door to the internationalization of the RMB. The existing international monetary order is centered on the U.S. dollar. As the issuing unit of the U.S. dollar, the Federal Reserve Board of the United States does everything possible to maintain the stability of the U.S. dollar to ensure the hegemony of the U.S. dollar. Whether it is asking the Organization of Petroleum Exporting Countries to force all oil-buying countries to use U.S. dollars for settlement, or the United States through the

implementation of international aid to expand the global influence of the U.S. dollar. The purpose is to ensure that the power to impose a U.S. dollar currency tax (seigniorage) will not be challenged.

U.S. e-commerce companies are aware of the broad prospects for the development of digital currency and decided to develop their digital currency. However, at a hearing held in the U.S. Senate, U.S. members of Congress attacked the issuance of digital currency by e-commerce companies. Although U.S. e-commerce companies possess advanced technology, they were forced to abandon their allocation under pressure from the U.S. Congress. Digital currency efforts. "The green hills can't cover it; after all, it will flow eastward."

It now appears that to maintain its sovereignty, the Federal Reserve Board has to consider issuing digital currency. However, it is complicated for the U.S. Federal Reserve to balance vested interest groups, modify the legal system of the U.S. Federal Reserve, and bypass the existing credit system to establish a secure digital currency system. For this reason the U.S. commercial bank is not a savings bank but a credit bank. The U.S. China (Hong Kong Stock 00370) Er Street Investment Bank obtains benefits by issuing bank cards and collecting loan interest. If digital currency is given, then the U.S. investment bank must change its business strategy and even adjust its business model and structure. Whether the U.S. Federal Reserve can overcome domestic difficulties and issue a secure digital currency based on the coordination of various interests requires further observation. However, one thing is sure: China will surely step up its efforts in the issuance of digital currency and lead most countries in the World.

SCOPE AND CONSEQUENCES OF THE DCEP FOR CHINA

The impact of transforming China into a cashless country will be positive on the one hand. Especially since today, almost 50% of the Chinese population makes their daily economic expenses using digital media.

In fact, more than 80% of smartphone users use their mobile devices to pay for point-of-sale transactions on a regular basis. This means that China has the highest mobile payment adoption rate in the World. It has even surpassed countries like South Korea and Japan, who held this place.

In this sense, the impact of DCEP in China will be relatively little. Society is used to digital payments and the wallets that they will use to manage DCEP will be natively integrated with the new currency making the transaction very simple. But on the contrary, there is everything that we have mentioned before. Everything you do with the currency will be monitored and subject to political decisions. Instead, they use of Bitcoin, or stable coin without fiat collateral like DAI, are better freedom solutions for everyone.

THE BENEFITS OF VIRTUAL CURRENCY FOR CHINA

Accordingly, it is perceived that China's principle objective is the advancement of Blockchain innovation is to utilize it as a device for public glorification. To catalyze its economy and a constituent component of an ideal worldwide matchless quality.

Furthermore, this is along these lines, on account of the unmistakable advantages that blockchains would bring to the nation and its administration. Beginning, obviously, with the internationalization of the Yuan, as its virtualization would permit the Chinese government to push its public money across fringes. It was running its Blockchain as an equal stage to SWIFT (the customary global financial framework), controlled by the One Belt One Road activity.

This would have the potential additionally to turn into a system for installments between organizations. All things considered, if right now WePay, WeChat's virtual installment stage, is the most widely recognized technique for exchanges between individuals. Virtualization has not been as productive as to associations, something the virtual government money could help with.

The administration blockchain could likewise give the legislature more noteworthy authority over food and medication entering the nation and keeping up observation through the Blockchain on the condition of food and the realness of the medications that enter and travel through the nation.

CHINA'S FIGHT AGAINST THE US

Talking about China being a world power, and the largest economy in the World, with an annual increase in GDP under normal circumstances of around 7%. China, at the time of imposing this virtual currency to companies and individuals, will obtain tax efficiency. Businesses will pay what they have to pay, and individuals will pay what they have to pay. That is, there will be no tax avaoidance. And the use, they can impose it.

They can do it the hard way, or the right way, offering advantages with its service, but in the end, whoever does not accept it for goodwill have to take it the hard way.

This will make the use of the Virtual Yuan grow, and cross borders. Right now, the Yuan does not have much impact internationally, but this could change if the Virtual Yuan offers a comfortable, practical and safe option. And of course, if it succeeds, it will eat ground from the U.S. dollar. This will not happen overnight, but if it is achieved, it will allow China to interact with many other countries without having to go through the Dollar. This will downplay the Dollar, and make the Virtual Yuan necessary.

We cannot forget that the Dollar is the World's leading currency. About ⅔ of the reserve assets of the World's central banks are denominated in dollars. And according to the SWIFT platform, 44% of registered international transactions were made in dollars. 30% in euros and China appears fifth at only 2%.

But if the Virtual Yuan gains popularity and begins to be used more, it would make it climb positions and therefore reduce the strength of the Dollar. We are not talking about it being loaded, but it could certainly take a lot of power.

In the end, what China seeks is to skip as much as possible everything that has to do with the United States. If you use your currency, the United States is as if it had it by the eggs, but if China can do everything it wants without having to go through the United States, things change. China would have more power and the United States less. If we add to this that China makes agreements with India, Brazil, or many other countries, they will further strengthen their currency.

But above all, if China's digital currency worked, there would be a war between currencies, since they would be fighting for the financial world power of the U.S. since the Virtual Yuan would not be related to the U.S. dollar.

Then we must also take into account that China has the BSN, the Blockchain Service Network, to which all countries could be associated, but, of course, having control, CHINA. Hence, to the extent that this progresses as the Chinese wish it to progress, it may be that power goes from being in the hands of the United States to be in less than China, hence, if everything goes well, China will get a lot of world power.

GLOSSARY

HNW: High Net Worth

CISI: Chartered Institute for Securities & Investment

CFA: Chartered Financial Analyst

MBA: Master of Business Administration

FINRA: Financial Industry Regulatory Authority

SME: Small to Medium Enterprise

DAI: Development Alternatives, Inc.

DCEP: Digital Currency Electronic Payment

RMB: Renminbi

CIPS: China International Payment System

GPDR: General Data Protection Regulation

PboC: People's Bank of China

CBDCs: Central Bank Digital Currency

GDP: Gross domestic product

Printed in Great Britain
by Amazon